CONTENT

by Charly Haley

Published by The Child's World®
1980 Lookout Drive • Mankato, MN 56003-1705
800-599-READ • www.childsworld.com

Photographs ©: Shutterstock Images, cover,
1, 5, 6, 13; Anastasiia Markus/Shutterstock
Images, 9; Olesia Bilkei/Shutterstock
Images, 10; iStockphoto, 14, 22 (bottom
left), 22 (bottom right); ESB Professional/
Shutterstock Images, 17; Maen Zayyad/
Shutterstock Images, 19; Rob Hainer/
Shutterstock Images, 20; Daxiao Productions/
Shutterstock Images, 22 (top left); Laboo
Studio/Shutterstock Images, 22 (top right)

Design Elements: Shutterstock Images

ISBN Hardcover: 9781503828056
ISBN Paperback: 9781622434657
LCCN: 2018944227

Printed in the United States of America
PAO2395

ABOUT THE AUTHOR

Charly Haley is a writer and children's book editor who lives in Minnesota. Aside from reading and writing, she enjoys music, yoga, and spending time with friends and family.

CONTENTS

JOEL IS CONTENT

Today was a normal day for Joel. He went to school. He saw his friends. He played with his brother after school. Joel felt content.

Nothing **bothered** Joel today. Nothing exciting happened. It was a good day.

FEELING CONTENT

People feel content when they are having a good day. They feel happy. They might smile.

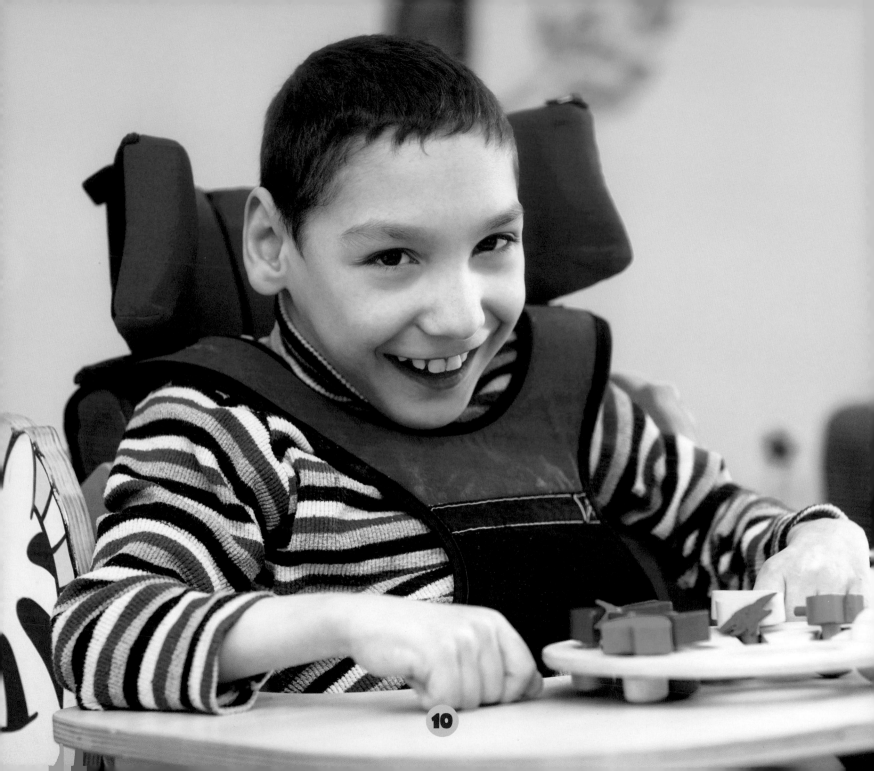

People who feel content are not **worried**.

They are not wishing something was better.

People who are content like
the way things are now.

THINK ABOUT IT

Can you think of a time when you felt content?

People who feel content might not show a lot of happiness. They might not laugh loudly. They might not jump up and down. But they feel good.

People who feel content might say they feel "fine" or "good." They use a **calm** voice. They do not sound mad or sad.

SEEING GOOD THINGS

People cannot always feel content.

Sometimes bad things happen.

Then people do not feel content.

It is okay to not feel content.

20

But when good things happen, it is good to **notice** them. Thinking about good things can help you feel content.

WHO IS CONTENT?

Can you tell who is content? Turn to page 24 for the answer.

GLOSSARY

bothered (BAH-therd) People feel bothered when something happens that they do not like. When Jane didn't get a toy she wanted, it bothered her.

calm (KALM) To be calm is to feel relaxed and at peace. Coloring can help you feel calm.

notice (NO-tiss) To notice something is to see it. Ava wanted people to notice her new shoes.

worried (WOR-eed) People are worried when something bad happens or when they think something bad will happen. Tommy was worried when his dog ran away.

TO LEARN MORE

Books

Dinmont, Kerry. ***Dan's First Day of School: A Book about Emotions***. Mankato, MN: The Child's World, 2018.

Millar, Goldie. ***F is for Feelings***. Minneapolis, MN: Free Spirit Publishing, 2014.

Nilsen, Genevieve. ***Happy***. Minneapolis, MN: Jump!, Inc., 2018.

Web Sites

Visit our Web site for links about being content:
childsworld.com/links

Note to Parents, Teachers, and Librarians: We routinely verify our Web links to make sure they are safe and active sites. So encourage your readers to check them out!

INDEX